I0164120

THE MIGHTY POWER OF THE WORD

Other Books by S. Richard Nelson

Turning Faith into Power

Gaining Power through Prayer

The Added Power of Obedience

The Healing Power of Forgiveness

The Gift and Power of the Holy Spirit

Love: The Only True Power

Sustainable Spirituality

The Faith Factor

5-star reviews are a blessing to Christian authors. If you find this book inspirational, educational or simply enjoyable, please post an honest review.

The Powerful Christian Series - Book V

THE MIGHTY POWER OF THE WORD

By S. Richard Nelson

Copyright © 2019 by Broken Hill Publications

All rights reserved. Except as permitted under the United States Copyright Act of 1976, and in the case of brief quotations embodied in critical articles and reviews, no part of this publication may be copied, reproduced or distributed in any form or by any means, or stored in a database or retrieval system, without the prior written authorization from the publisher.

First Edition published 2019

ISBN-13: 978-0-9904973-9-4
ISBN-10: 0-9904973-9-9
BISAC: Religion / Christian Life / Spiritual Growth

Broken Hill Publications
Glenwood Springs, CO 81601

Artistic Design by Connie & Stephen Gorton

"From this broken hill,
All your praises they shall ring."

L. Cohen – If It Be Your Will

www.srnelson.com

"For God did not give us a Spirit of fear but of power and love and self-control."

2 Timothy 1:7 (NET)

Table of Contents

"Life is peaceful when we rest on the promises of God's word."

Chapter 1

The Power of Words

Paul declared, "The sword of the Spirit ... is the word of God." (Ephesians 6:17) Throughout the Bible we are reminded of the impressive power of words.

God spoke four simple words, "Let there be light," and there was light.

Joshua's powerful words caused the sun to stand still.

Elijah used words to command that no rain should fall.

Jesus Christ explained the righteous power of words that are coupled with faith: "If you have faith the size of a mustard seed, you will say to this mountain, 'move from here to there,' and it will move." (Matthew 17:20)

The entire nature and character of Saul of Tarsus was altered by the words, "Saul, Saul, why are you persecuting me?" (Acts 9:4)

Forever changed and converted by this experience, the Apostle Paul wrote about the importance of hearing the word of

God: "So, faith comes by hearing, and hearing by the word of God." (Romans 10:17)

There is a mighty power in words. They contain the ability to remove fear, to comfort hearts, to revive our spirit, to refresh our soul and to enlighten our understanding. Take a moment to reflect on the experiences you have had with words. Were you ever touched and comforted by the words of a friend? Were you ever uplifted by the inspiring words of a powerful song? Did the rousing words of an influential teacher or minister ever motivate you to action? Did the promising words from a Bible verse ever cause a dramatic change in your heart and character?

Paul describes the word of God as "piercing" as well as "living." It is precision combined with power. It is "sharper than any double-edged sword, piercing even to the point of dividing soul from spirit, and joints from marrow; It is able to judge the desires and thoughts of the heart." (Hebrews 4:12)

There is purity as well as power in the word of God. The word of God is powerful enough that those who preach, teach and witness do not need to carry the burden of converting their listeners. Sinners are turned in their tracks and changed in their hearts through servants of God who witness to them in righteous testimony.

The words of scripture are not the words of men, but of God. The words of men may be witty but they're rarely wise; they can be clever but they're seldom substantial. The word of

God, on the other hand, can go straight to the heart. They are the words of Christ and his word can have a powerful effect on human intellect and emotion.

As Paul explained to the Corinthians: "When I came to you, brothers and sisters, I did not come with superior eloquence or wisdom as I proclaimed the testimony of God. For I decided to be concerned about nothing among you except Jesus Christ and him crucified. And I was with you in weakness and in fear and with much trembling. My conversation and my preaching were not with persuasive words of wisdom, but with a demonstration of the Spirit and of power, so that your faith would not be based on human wisdom but on the power of God." (1 Corinthians 2:1-5)

The words of God can give us rock-like stability and firmness in turbulent and troubled times, especially in this day and age when the entire world seems to be in commotion. Our minds and our spirits can be sharpened by the scriptures. The word of God can be like pointers in a compass that guide us through the trials of life and indicate for us the direction we should follow to find forgiveness and security.

The prolific Christian writer, C. S. Lewis explained and cautioned that history has revealed to us how individual people as well as entire cultures and civilizations fall into the incongruous and ironic ruse of anxiously running around with fire extinguishers in times of flood. The words of God—studied, practiced and applied—can be a lifeboat.

The Bible can ensure that we will think more about Jesus every day of our lives. The words of God can move us away from a lamentable life of living and experiencing the cares and concerns of the world. Through a familiarity with the word of God, the Savior will no longer be a stranger to us, far from the thoughts and intents of our hearts, but will, instead, become a close and comforting friend.

God told Moses to "write down these words, for in accordance with these words I have made a covenant with you and with Israel." (Exodus 34:27) Throughout the Bible, God reminds us of the power of his word.

The power we find in the word of God is not contained in sophisticated and eloquent language that appeals to the wise and educated people of the world. The power flows from the pure and simple word of God to anyone willing to receive it. "Our gospel did not come to you merely in words, but in power and in the Holy Spirit and with deep conviction." (1 Thessalonians 1:5)

Reading and studying the Holy Scriptures will place us in a position to experience the life-changing power and the virtue of the word of God. Through an active practice of reading and then applying what we read, Jesus can remain constantly in our thoughts and become our close friend and companion.

"I treated [the Bible] as one treats a priceless possession, a thing of great value, a rare treasure.... It gave me strength and assurance."

A Prisoner held behind the Iron Curtain

Chapter 2

The Treasure House

Millions of books exist in the world today, and new books are being published and sold every day. It would be impossible for anyone to read them all. James Chapman recently created a list of the most read books in the world. He based his findings on the number of copies each book sold over the last 50 years.

Chapman discovered that the Bible far outsold any other book. Bibles sales reached a staggering 3.9 billion copies over the last 50 years. (Second place goes to "Quotations from the Works of Mao Tse-tung" selling 820 million copies, and third place goes to the immensely popular "Harry Potter" series with 400 million copies sold.)

The Bible, the account of God's dealings with his children in the world and his purpose with all creation, still remains the most popular and most read book in the world today. The Bible is a remarkable collection of sixty-six books containing the messages of God and is among the most important books and writings on the earth today.

Tens of thousands who have read it are firmly convinced and testify that the Bible embodies the mind and will of God. It also contains historical information concerning the reactions of earlier peoples to the teachings of God.

After God revealed his truths to his prophets, he commanded the prophets to record these revelations for the benefit of future generations. He then holds us responsible for reading and living what is taught and written by these prophets. The Bible—the will, mind, word, and voice of God—is the measuring rod by which everything else is judged. The truth of all things is measured by the scriptures.

The Bible is a treasure house with countless rooms containing gems to bless and enrich our earthly existence. An amazing aspect of this treasure house is that each time we search the various rooms we can uncover additional riches.

Treasures discovered in the Bible can help us resolve personal problems.

Treasures buried in the Bible can help us make correct choices based on an eternal understanding.

Treasures contained in the Bible can help us learn from the mistakes of past generations so that we can improve our own situation and standing with God.

Treasures revealed in the Bible testify of God the Father and of his Son, Jesus Christ, who is our Savior and Redeemer.

Treasures uncovered in the Bible contain the teachings that will return us to the presence of God.

To those who accept it, the Bible is a signpost along the trail of life pointing out the direction we should travel. To those who have not accepted it, the Bible is a lighthouse on the shore of turbulent seas beckoning safe passage to a secure harbor.

Regardless of how many times you have read the Bible, read it again. The lessons you will learn each time you read this great book will help you find an answer to some problem you are tackling.

In the New Testament both Matthew and Mark recount when the Sadducees asked Christ a question concerning the writings of Moses. They wanted to know if a man married his brother's widow, whose wife would she be in the Resurrection. Jesus answered, "You are mistaken, not knowing the scriptures, nor the power of God." (Matthew 22:29; Mark 12:24) We should read the Bible to gain a greater concept of the power of God and an increased understanding of his ways.

Satan does not want us to read the Bible because he does not want us to have that greater concept and understanding. If we seriously study the Bible, we just might learn that God is our Father and that Jesus is the Christ, the divine Son of God. Satan doesn't want that. If we diligently seek for the valuable hidden treasures buried within the verses of biblical writings, we might uncover the gospel principles of happiness and improvement that offer everlasting joy and eternal life.

The devil does not want us to have these treasures and he will do everything he can to prevent our discovery by stopping us from reading and studying the mighty word of God.

We should resolutely decide to read, study and meditate on the word of God and then stick firmly to that resolution. We should have a regular program of daily Bible study as a family, with friends or just by ourselves.

Biblical illiteracy is a significant cause of complaints among today's Christian fellowship. The Old Testament tells of a time in the last days when "those who complain will acquire insight." It is useful to examine a few verses of scripture that address complaining among believers. When Christians and others are not acquainted with the ways of the Lord, they tend to grumble and complain.

The children of Israel seemed to complain constantly because they did not have the same spiritual insight and understanding given to Moses.

"And all the Israelites murmured against Moses and Aaron: and the whole congregation said to them, 'If only we had died in the land of Egypt! or if only we had perished in this wilderness!'" (Numbers 14:2)

If the children of Israel had understood what Moses knew about their exodus to the promised land, perhaps they would not have complained. The scribes and Pharisees in Jesus' time also seemed to have plenty to complain about.

"But the Pharisees and the experts in the law were complaining, 'This man welcomes sinners and eats with them.'" (Luke 15:2)

The Pharisees and scribes complained because they could not understand that Christ came to save sinners. John relates that, although the Jews could understand that manna had been sent from heaven to save ancient Israel from starvation and temporal death, they did not understand that the bread which Christ would give was his flesh.

"Then the Jews who were hostile to Jesus began complaining about him because he said, 'I am the bread that came down from heaven.'" (John 6:41)

The Jews complained because they did not understand this doctrine, and many of the Savior's disciples felt that this was "a difficult saying" and "quit following him and did not accompany him any longer." (John 6:60, 66)

The Bible represents the spiritual memory of humankind. When we disengage from our connection with the scriptures, we suffer a disastrous denial of the knowledge and awareness of that vast spiritual history handed down from the very beginning of this world, the very beginning of life on planet earth. The Bible is the life preserver of the magnificent principles of God's great kingdom on earth.

Faith is born from a sincere and significant study of the scriptures. The passage into the sacred treasure house is unlocked through studying the Bible and praying about its message and significance. By seeking to understand its deep and hidden meanings, we can receive an outpouring of light and knowledge from the Holy Spirit. The development of faith is a direct result of scripture study.

"The grass withers, the flower fades, but the word of our God will stand forever."

Isaiah 40:8

Chapter 3

A Powerful Force Unleashed

While it is wonderful to think that the Bible is the most popular book in the world, it wasn't always so. Powerful progress has been made since the first printed Bibles appeared, especially in overcoming the depths to which early Christian religions once sank, where depravity and ignorance were prevalent and widespread among religious leaders, and the word of God was kept secret, hidden from the common population of the world. Printing the Bible in the influential languages of the sixteenth century and making it readily available to the common population unleashed a powerful force on earth.

The pronounced impact of this powerful force began with the Reformation and from there spread through all the subsequent centuries with wider influence than we can imagine.

In Western civilization, the Bible has been the principal tool of persuasion in humanity's pursuit to purify religion—to uncover the buried treasures of truth within the sacred writings. A theological and biblical stimulus has provided an inspirational light and a leavening influence in the hearts of sincere Christians all over the world.

Another impact of this powerful force, too often attributed to political persuasion, is in the encouraging, nurturing and sustaining of the spirit of liberty and independence stimulated and strengthened through the Bible. The desire and drive for civil liberties and freedom are linked to and interwoven with our early pursuit for religious freedom. Determined to pursue the freedom to worship God as directed in the Bible, the Puritans became the first effective settlers in the New World. They were the first of many who, driven by the same desire, found their way to America. My own great-grandfather, ten generations before me, inscribed in his journal, *"I left England for the sole purpose of finding religious freedom."*

Freedom of religion emerges among the first freedoms established by our founding fathers. "Congress shall make no law respecting an establishment of religion, or prohibiting the free exercise thereof; or abridging the freedom of speech, or of the press; or the right of the people peaceably to assemble, and to petition the Government for a redress of grievance." [i]

The Bible has exerted a mighty power on the hearts of some of our greatest leaders to venerate and to defend our freedoms. Among those leaders this nation's first president,

George Washington, asserted that "it is impossible to rightly govern the world without God and the Bible." [ii]

President Woodrow Wilson firmly believed that the destiny of America lies directly tied to daily Bible study. He stated: "I ask every man and woman in this audience that from this day on they will realize that part of the destiny of America lies in their daily perusal of this great book." [iii] I wonder if there are any political leaders today who recognize that they, along with every American citizen, must draw their strength, guidance and inspiration from the Bible if freedom is to be preserved.

Ironically, the greatest indication, perhaps, of the power of the Bible is how severely it is criticized and condemned by non-believers. Antagonists who claim the Bible is no more than a collection of fables and fairy tales cannot justify or explain why it remains banned in over fifty countries throughout the world. None of Aesop's Fables are banned.

Hitler believed the Bible to be such a great threat to his objectives and aspirations that he sought to alter the New Testament and to destroy the Old Testament. [iv] He commented that, "Whether it is the Old Testament or the New, or simply the sayings of Jesus, it is all the same old Jewish swindle." [v] Yet the Bible remained a powerful strength throughout Europe and the world. "The Bible was the weapon of our souls," commented one prisoner of war. "It was with us in suffering, it fought for us, and our foes feared it. Why did they hate that very old book? For the same reasons we ourselves loved it. The Bible spoke to us as a voice closer to our trembling hearts than any other voice." [vi]

This constant struggle over Biblical veracity continues today. Many countries throughout the world deny the truthfulness of this powerful book. The very word of God is officially characterized and labeled as an "unscientific collection of fantastic legends," and a "tool of imperialistic, capitalistic powers for subjugating backward, unknowing nations." But these same arguments and criticisms against it are a witness of its potency and power, and the Bible remains accepted and embraced with stirring loyalty by its believers worldwide.

Perhaps the greatest influence the Bible has had since it became available to the world is the effect it has had on the moral character of its readers. The powerful impact of the word of God, the message of humanity's divine creation, the advent of the birth of God's Son, the Savior's powerful teachings of love, humility and kindness, and the greatest eternal love story ever told that Jesus Christ would take the burden of our sins and give his life for us are circulating with ever increasing speed to the darkest corners of the earth.

All those who accept and observe the truths of biblical teachings experience a change for the better. Centuries ago John Richard Greene wrote of the profound sway and influence the Bible had on the citizens of Great Britain: "No greater moral change ever passed over a nation than passed over England.

England became the people of a book, and that book was the Bible.... Far greater than its effect on literature or social phrase was the effect of the Bible on the people at large. The whole temper of the nation felt the change. A new conception of life and of man superseded the old. A new moral and religious impulse spread through every class." [vii]

That incredible power and influential force continues throughout the world today.

Despite the recurrent war raging against the word of God throughout the modern world, an ongoing labor of love to make the Bible accessible to everyone throughout the world in every language persists. Collaborations of numerous Christian organizations toil to take translated Bibles to every nation everywhere, an overwhelming ambition and objective that deserves our praise, prayers and appreciation.

Mention should be made also, and prayers of gratitude offered, to the numerous dedicated individuals and groups from various Christian denominations who conscientiously endeavor to bring greater validity and comprehension to the claims made in the Bible. Archaeologists continuously sift through sand and ruins, scouring ancient deserts for ever more enlightening evidences regarding the people of the Bible. Biblical scholars perfect their comprehension of original languages to better decipher the ancient teachings God has given us through the Bible. Certainly, in any arena of research, we come across occasional misinterpretations, mistakes and misunderstandings, but the Bible and its profound and divine teachings persistently enlarge the perception and perspective of people everywhere. The great sacrifices achieved throughout history in making the Bible available to all inspires tremendous gratitude for the scriptures we have available in our homes and in our churches. The word of God, in any language, is "useful for teaching, for reproof, for correction, and for training in righteousness: that the person dedicated to God may be capable and equipped for every good work." (2 Timothy 3:16-17)

"Don't declare that God is silent if your Bible is shut."

Chapter 4

Hearing the Lord's Voice

Perhaps the greatest blessing offered us through the Bible is the power it gives us to hear the voice of the Lord. This is the principle and primary reason for reading the scriptures. Through our reading we can hear the voice of the Lord instructing, guiding, and communicating deep feelings of peace and love through the Holy Spirit. Everyone who reads the word of God with a pure, humble heart will hear the sweet whisperings of the Lord's voice.

Paul explains that "faith comes by hearing, and hearing by the word of God." (Romans 10:17) How to hear the voice of the Lord is one of the most important concepts we can glean from reading the Bible. Beyond mere reading, inspiration, instruction and insight come when we prayerfully contemplate God's words. God will speak to us "between the lines." He will address our current problems while we are studying the content of his words. Studying the Bible opens the door to direction from God. Scripture study is the most effective tool available for communicating with God.

So, what must we do in order to feel the spiritual impressions and divine enlightenment in our minds and in our hearts? It is not difficult to learn to hear the voice of the Lord as we read and study the Bible, but it does take a measure of mastery and discipline. (Remember that discipline has the same root meaning as disciple.) Following a simple, four-step procedure will help us hear the Lord's voice as we read the Bible.

Step One: Prepare yourself through the power of prayer.

Praying in faith—not just once in a while, but every time we read, will fine-tune us in to the Spirit of God. When God attempts to speak to us through the Bible and by the power of his Spirit, unless we have prepared our hearts and minds, we may not perceive his voice. If we prepare ourselves through prayer, God will speak to us because we ask. This is not just something we should do occasionally, but whenever we study God's words.

We cannot read the Bible the same way we read other books. The Bible must be prayed over, and we must be humble if we want to hear the Lord's voice speaking to us. Prayer has enormous power to create and open a spiritual communication during our Bible studies. Then, if we want to hear God's voice and have his wisdom fill our hearts, we need to be humble.

Step Two: Prepare yourself by being humble.

If we will recall and consider God's mercies and humble ourselves before we read our scriptures, we will be better prepared to hear the voice of the Lord. We should remember and recognize how merciful Jesus is to us in our sins. When we recognize how dependent we are on God for all our gifts and blessings our hearts should fill with unspeakable gratitude. We should consider our blessings and how patient and merciful God is with us in our sins and how quick he is to forgive. The better we become at being humble and praying, the more God will enrich our understanding. When we pray and humble ourselves, we will hear the voice of the Lord in our studies. When we do fill our hearts with gratitude and are humble, we are in a perfect position to hear God's voice as we seek, search and study.

Step Three: Don't just read; seek, search and study.

We need to think about what we are reading, constantly asking God for answers and direction. We can highlight words and verses that are impressionable to our hearts and cross-reference them with other verses. If we are serious about hearing the

Lord's voice, we can and should write down the principles and truths we receive when we are studying. We should memorize verses that are particularly important and impactful to us.

When we memorize a scripture and repeat it in our minds throughout the day, God will aid us in affecting that truth in our day-to-day lives. And, of course, we need to put into practice the principles we pick up as we study and ponder.

Step Four: Practice the principles.

When we incorporate the principles of truth into our daily pattern of living as we discover them in our Bible studies, God will continue to enlighten us and teach us greater truths. On the other hand, if God teaches us a new principle or a new truth and we do not change our behavior because of it, he will be less likely to share greater truth with us.

An effective way to incorporate principles of truth is to share them with other people. It has been said that if we cannot share truth with someone else, then we do not really know it or own it. In other words, we may think we fully understand something but until we can teach it to someone else, we very likely don't understand it that well ourselves. If we can share it and help another person to understand it, then we are likely able to learn and understand even more.

This simple, four-step procedure will help us hear the Lord's voice as we read the Bible. When we follow this process to pray, humble ourselves, search and then obey the principles we learn and discover, we can be assured that the voice of the Lord is speaking to us. The words of the Bible will have a greater influence and effect in our everyday living, and we will see our faith grow and our hearts embrace the word of God with increased understanding. But we must take the initiative and follow these steps, or we will not hear his voice.

For the same reason that we don't teach calculous to kindergarteners, God does not teach all his truths to us all at once. His pattern for teaching his children is "precept on precept; line on line; ... here a little, there a little." (Isaiah 28:10) So be patient. God's answers are always based on his love for us. If he gave us too much new wisdom and we couldn't follow it or obey, our added wisdom would become a burden instead of a blessing. To help us grow, God gives us a little bit here and a little bit there. Once we can apply a new truth in our lives, he will give us more. In order to hear more of the Lord's voice, we need to obey the words we have already heard from him. We need to demonstrate to God that we believe his word is worth our time, attention and effort.

I love what I read in the Bible. I love being taught by God when I am willing to make the time and the effort to hear his voice. His teaching is the greatest. Any problem or difficulty we face can be solved through God's word. When I read the scriptures daily, my day just goes better.

"The longer the tea bag sits in the cup, the stronger the tea. The more God's Word saturates our minds, the clearer our grasp of what's important to Him."

Joni Eareckson Tada

Chapter 5

The Blessings of Bible Study

Considering what a powerful privilege and blessing the Bible brings to us, why does it often seem so difficult to consistently and conscientiously read it? We seem to struggle, for the most part, as individuals and families, to read God's word as frequently or as regularly as we should. Often unavoidable obstacles impede our progress in developing consistent Bible study habits.

Jesus tells us that no one can serve two masters. He voluntarily submitted to the will of his Father. In our human state, we often pit our will against the will of our Father and struggle between choosing good works over bad.

Our busy and demanding lifestyles are often a burden to effective Bible study. Little things get in the way and we fail to see the forest for the trees; we fail to see how studying the word of God would help take care of those little things. The Bible has the answers to our daily struggles.

In his writings Peter mentions people who "stumble at the word." (1 Peter 2:8) Today the ideologies, philosophies and wisdom of the world seem to be overtaking the teachings and the word of God.

Sometimes it's just difficult to understand or appreciate how lessons, stories, and examples from more than two thousand years ago can really speak to the problems and difficulties of today. We may read the words but not fully understand the message.

Egotism can be a problem for some of us. We are afraid to admit that we don't understand some of what we are reading, and we don't want others to realize how much we don't know. But then our spiritual growth is stymied. If we humble ourselves before we study God's word, we can better understand it, enjoy it, and grow from the experience.

A major reason we fail to study the Bible as much as we should is because we haven't decided that it is important enough to do so. We fail to make the decision to study God's word at any cost. If we truly understood the importance of Bible study, we would make it a foundation for our daily lives.

Another impediment that comes to mind is television. We sometimes become so involved in streaming and binge watching our favorite television shows that there isn't time to read the word of God.

Some of us may feel intimidated by the language of the Bible. The phraseology may appear odd and outdated to us.

Or, if we were raised in a Cristian family, we may feel that we've heard it all before, from our parents, from our Pastors, from our Summer Bible Camp Leaders. It may feel like it's just the same old stuff we've heard all our lives.

Maybe the Bible is just too much to read or maybe we read it but forget what we've read. Some people think the ancient writing of the Bible is dry and boring when in reality reading the scriptures can be enlightening, inspiring and enjoyable. The lessons from the scriptures can teach us valuable principles and ideas that will benefit us every day of our lives. They are instructions from heaven to us on the earth. They can teach us how we can return to our heavenly home. Bible study will help us:

1. Find Jesus Christ.
2. Obtain answers to our prayers.
3. Be humble and kind.
4. Increase our faith.
5. Repent of our sins.
6. Learn good values.
7. Solve life's problems.
8. Stay focused on the Lord.

The list goes on and on.

When the Bible is not being studied as it should, our homes are weakened. When we reject the word of God in our lives or replace it with worldly entertainment, teachings and trends, we lose the anchor of the scriptures and drift easily into corruption and are then drawn away by the enticement of the world.

From my experience the concerns mentioned earlier are relatively common to many Christians. Honestly, I've used some of them myself, but in the end, they seem to be closer to excuses than genuine reasons for laying aside the word of God. I believe that most of the excuses we invent for not reading the Bible can all be encapsulated in two basic pretexts.

The first reason we have difficulty studying the Bible is unbelief. It appears that many Christians lack the explicit belief that the Bible will provide any real answers to the troubles weighing them down. Perhaps they feel the promises are not literal. Or they doubt that the messages, assurances and counsel contained in the Bible are actually the word of God. In either case, it becomes a question of faith.

The second reason entails a question of pride. When we feel we know enough already, we stop searching for more answers. On the other hand, if we are embarrassed by how little we know of God's Word and how inexperienced we are at researching scripture, we may pretend that we know enough already and not look for added guidance or direction from God.

A lack of faith or an abundance of pride stop many Christians today from delving into the word of God. We may view and voice our objections differently, but the center of these objections almost always involves one of these two basic pretexts.

Timothy tells us the value and the purpose of God's word: "From infancy, you have known the sacred writings which are able to make you wise to salvation through faith, which is in Christ Jesus. Every scripture inspired by God is also profitable for teaching, for reproof, for correction, for instruction which is in righteousness, that the man of God may be complete, furnished completely to every good work." (2 Timothy 3:15-17)

Jesus tells us that "the wind blows wherever it will, and you hear the sound it makes, but do not know where it comes from or where it is going. So it is with everyone who is born of the spirit." (John 3:8) The Spirit speaks to us and works in us in many different ways, but the result is always the same.

Family Bible study can be a powerful tool for having the Holy Spirit speak to us. It is a wonderful blessing for parents and for their children. Love, harmony and comprehension in Christ's gospel will increase as parents read the word of God together with their children. What could better turn the hearts of children to their parents or the hearts of parents to their children, for that matter, than a rich, vibrant declaration of heaven witnessed by the Holy Spirit?

Without the words written in the Bible, parents would never be able to remember all the vital teachings that God wants us to share with our children. When we study the Bible thoroughly and methodically, everything we need to better teach, instruct and counsel our children is laid out for us. And God himself has provided the content.

Don't worry if you can't remember everything you read. Jesus told us that "the Comforter, even the Holy Spirit, whom the Father will send in my name, he shall teach you all things, and bring to your remembrance all that I said unto you." (John 14:26) If you grapple to remember the words of the Bible, you can ask God specifically for help with your Bible learning. He offers the beautiful promise that he will help you learn, apply and internalize the scriptures you are reading—and he will help you to remember what he is teaching you.

When you begin to study the word of God together as a family, you will notice some miraculous changes. Any of the following could be included in these changes:

    📖 Family Bible study builds faith within the family.
    📖 Family Bible study engenders love within the family.
    📖 Family Bible study creates a daily focus on God and Jesus and all they have done for us.

- Family Bible study creates powerful "superheroes" our children can admire and emulate.
- Family Bible study gives families a time to be together in an intense and busy world.
- Family Bible study is an effective way to worship God together.
- Family Bible study allows children to raise questions or concerns they could be facing at school or with friends and then, answers to their concerns can be sought in the scriptures.
- Family Bible study in the morning begins our day with a spiritual blessing.
- Family Bible study at night ends our day with gratitude toward God.
- Family Bible study allows parents to share and discuss values and morals they wish to instill in their children.
- Family Bible study allows the Spirit to witness to all family members together at the same time.
- Family Bible study creates a time for listening, sharing and understanding.

The list of benefits and blessings from family Bible study is extensive. If parents will read from the Bible prayerfully and regularly, both by themselves and with their children, the Holy

Spirit will permeate their homes. Peace and tranquility will fill their walls and contention will decrease. Love, respect and consideration for each other will grow. Faith will also increase, and the love of Christ will flow and flourish bringing greater joy and happiness into their homes.

Perhaps one of the greatest benefits and blessings of family Bible study is that it brings the family together. When our learning, knowledge and understanding are centered in the word of God we become more effective in all our efforts.

Satan does not want us to study God's Word. He will do all he can to stop us, putting obstacles in our way constantly. But our God is stronger and, if we persist, God will reward our efforts. If children support their parents and parents pray for their children, then our family Bible study can remove evil influences and bring peace and comfort into our homes.

We shouldn't take the word of God for granted. His word is one of the most valuable gifts he has given us. Make a recommitment to study the Bible. Immerse yourself in the word of God daily. Read the scriptures with your children and teach your children to love and treasure the Bible. Then seek and follow the guidance of the Holy Spirit to encourage your friends and acquaintances to do the same.

The advice given in Deuteronomy 17:19 counsels that we should keep the scriptures with us constantly, read from them all the days of our lives, so that we may learn to revere the Lord our God and observe *all* the words of this law and these statutes and do them.

The more you study the word of God, the better you will be able to judge between Christ and anti-Christ. You will have increased power to do good and to resist evil. You will gain a better understanding of God's word and his will. If you will feast from the lavish fortune found in the pages of the Lord's treasure house, God will satisfy your soul with a wealth of blessings like you have never known before.

"I receive more true knowledge from reading the book of God in one month than I could ever have acquired from all the writings of men."

George Whitefield

Chapter 6

A Powerful Feast

"Your word is truth." (John 17:17)

The bell-ringers of falsehood and blasphemy are clanging on every corner today. The philosophies of human intellect are seen as greater than the wisdom of our loving God. Science is seen as sacred, seeking a higher standing than scripture and faith is confused for fantasy. So much effort is expended in worldly education while the word of God gathers dust on our bookshelves.

What our wanton world really needs today is to invest time in partaking from the powerful feast God has laid before us. Reading and studying the Bible is not a burden for Christians but an abundant blessing and opportunity. Arthur W. Pink, one of the most influential evangelical authors in the second half of the twentieth century, stated that "the Bible is no lazy man's book! Much of its treasure, like the valuable minerals stored in the bowels of the earth, only yield up themselves to the diligent seeker."

Millions of Christians throughout the world turn to the Bible in their hour of greatest need and are edified, instructed, and encouraged. They are granted direction and comfort in moments for doubt and insecurity. The Book of Psalms is a feast for the soul in distress. Through a sincere study of God's word everyone can come to know Jesus the Christ.

God told Israel's great prophet-leader Joshua: "This book of the law shall not depart out of your mouth; but you shall meditate thereon day and night, that you may observe to do according to all that is written therein: for then you shall make your way prosperous, and then you shall have good success." (Joshua 1:8) God was assuring Joshua that his life would prosper and that he would have success in those things that matter most in life. The more acquainted and conversant we are with the Bible, the better we understand the mind of God and see his direction for our lives. God's eternal truth will be set firmly into our hearts and minds. We need not wander in darkness. The Bible is our guiding light. Its message is illuminating lives throughout the world.

The Bible expounds the great love God has for his children and it teaches of the atoning sacrifice of our Savior. It tells us how we should live and offers us a way to enter the heavenly mansions prepared for us. The word of God imparts the wisdom, knowledge and power to improve our lives and directs us through times of trouble. Everyone who will prayerfully and judiciously search and study the pages of the Bible will find comfort, counsel, guidance, and the quiet influence of the Holy Spirit to help bring greater power into their lives.

As a faithful Christian, do you treasure the word of God?

Are you using the books of the Bible to bless and improve your life?

Do you use the Scriptures as a shield against Satan?

The Bible was given to us for these very specific reasons. It contains the mind, the will and the words of God. It can be a weapon against wickedness, a comfort and consolation in times of turmoil, and a witness to the work and wonders of an Almighty God. Only an open and well-read Bible will reveal the voice of the Lord in your life.

Don't all of us need greater spirituality? Spirituality increases as we feast on the words of Christ. Adjust your efforts and bend your activities to include a meaningful and motivating study of God's word. When you do, whether individually, as a group or in a family, other areas of your life will improve. Your commitment to Christ will grow stronger, your witness of his work will increase, you will hear his word influencing your decisions and your faith will be fortified.   The way to develop greater spirituality is to feast on the words of Christ.

Study the Bible. Immerse yourself in the scriptures. Learn the doctrine and master the principles of the Gospel. Feast on the word of God. The invested effort will wield wonderous results and divine dividends. The word of God will fortify you and arm you with his Holy Spirit allowing you to resist evil, live righteously and feel joy in life. The Bible is one of the most valuable gifts given to us and we should receive it with gladness and solemnity.

- Recommit yourself to a regular study of the Bible.
- Immerse yourself in God's word daily.
- Read the Bible as a family and instill in your children a love of the scriptures.
- Encourage others to do the same.

Read and study both the Old and the New Testaments. They are a source of great truth. From their pages we learn of the hand of God in directing the lives of his people from the very beginning of earth's history. We learn the life and ministry of Christ. We cannot overestimate the impact the Bible has had on the people of the world. Its words have strengthened the faith of generations. That sacred and holy book, the number one best-seller of all time, is a treasure house of immeasurable worth to humanity.

America's founding fathers understood that "where the spirit of the Lord is present, there is freedom." (2 Corinthians 3:17) The United States of America commenced and continues through a rich faith in God. The Bible is the foundation for this faith. As quoted earlier in Chapter 3, it is impossible to rightly govern the world without God and the Bible, and it will be impossible to continue its governance without them as well.

The chief and central assertion of the Bible is that Jesus is the Christ, the promised Messiah, Lord and Redeemer. He redeemed us from a lost and fallen state occasioned by Adam's transgression. All Christian churches accept this truth as fundamental to their faith.

Today, much of the world discards the divinity of Jesus Christ. They mistrust the message of his miraculous birth, his faultless life, and the reality of his resurrection. The Bible teaches truth in unmistakable terms. Its primary purpose is to guide us to Christ to be reconciled with him. The sincere seeker of truth will surely realize that Jesus is the Christ by prayerfully pondering the inspired words of the Bible.

The Bible will bring us to Christ through two fundamental formulas.

First, it will teach us of Jesus and his gospel. It is a witness of his divine nature. It explains our need for a Redeemer and for putting our trust in him. It explicates the fall of Adam and the Atonement of Christ. It clarifies our need of a spiritual rebirth.

It proclaims that we should try to live the life of a Christian believer.

Second, the Bible unmasks the opponents of Christ. It foils and frustrates teachers of false doctrines. It sustains and strengthens the soldiers of Christ against the evil designs, doctrines and strategies of the devil in our day.

More and more people are being persuaded, through the Bible, that Jesus is the Christ. More of us now need to be persuaded to utilize the Bible to become more committed to Christ. We need to be convinced and committed. Return to a regular study of the Bible. Learn more about accepting Jesus and becoming committed to him, centered in him, and consumed in him.

The Bible must be re-enthroned in our hearts and in our minds. We must honor it by reading it, by studying it, by living its precepts and transforming our lives by becoming true followers of Christ. We shouldn't be complacent with just reading occasionally. As faithful Christians we should not be satisfied until we have read the Bible over and over again.

The more we teach and preach from the Bible, the more we will gratify God and the greater will be our power of preaching and witnessing to the world. This is how we will increase Christian converts throughout the world. It is our divine commission to teach the words of the gospel in the Bible.

Yesterday's dinner will not sustain today's need. Infrequently feasting on the word of God will not sustain our daily need for spiritual nourishment either. We cannot watch television for three hours and study the word of God for three minutes and still expect to grow spiritually. What better way to nourish the spirit than to frequently feast from the Bible?

The Bible provides us hope that can only come from God. The more you read the Bible, the more you will love the Author. With God's help we can do what is right.

"No one can read the Gospels without actually feeling the presence of Jesus. His personality pulsates in every word. No myth is filled with such life."

Albert Einstein
Saturday Evening Post,
October 26, 1929.

5-star reviews are a blessing to Christian authors. If you found this book inspirational, educational or simply enjoyable, please post an honest review.

About the Author

Rich Nelson is the author of a variety of published books and articles on topics such as religious education, family values, health, and politics. His work has appeared in *Christian Education Today, Church Teacher, Parish Teacher, Living with Teenagers, Liberty Magazine,* and many others.

Contact Information:
Broken Hill Publications
Glenwood Springs, CO 91601

Email Rich at: rich@srnelson.com

Visit Rich at: www.srnelson.com

Other Books by Rich Nelson

Turning Faith into Power

Book 1 in The Powerful Christian Series.

Turning Faith into Power is the first in a series of instructive and inspirational books from The Powerful Christian Series by S. Richard Nelson. The Savior says in Matthew 17:19-20, "For most assuredly I tell you, If you have faith as a grain of mustard seed, you will tell this mountain, move from here to there, and it will move; and nothing will be impossible to you."

What mountains would you remove from your life if you had the faith of a mustard seed?

What's stopping you from removing the obstacles in your life?

Do you utilize your faith as a principle of action and power?

Is your faith centered where it will be most effective?

Do you have adequate faith in yourself?

As believing Christians there is substantial power available to us. It is the power of faith. Through the bounteous mercy and love of Jesus Christ we receive his grace - a divine means of strength. The power available to us through Jesus Christ is very real.

Gaining Power through Prayer

Book 2 in The Powerful Christian Series

Sincere prayer is a fountain of divine power flowing into our lives. Through prayer we gain clear and precise direction. Through prayer we access the strength of character to perform God's will – to do what is right. Prayer is the process we use to place ourselves in contact with God.

The impressive power of prayer warrants the consideration not only of Christians, but of all societies. This little booklet highlights the principle applications and purposes of prayer. It confirms that God does answer our prayers and demonstrates how we can be more aware of those divine answers. It also examines the challenging question of why, at times, it appears that God does not answer us and what we can do about it.

The Added Power of Obedience

Book 3 in The Powerful Christian Series

Two opposing powers grapple in every human heart and our decisions are usually influenced by them, either to do good or to do evil. The spirit of truth will always persuade us to obey God. We all want happiness. We hope for it, live for it, and make it our primary goal in life. But do we live in a way that allows us to enjoy the happiness we desire so deeply?

The way to be happy is simply to believe in Jesus Christ and obey the gospel. When we obey God's law, then we can expect to find the happiness we desire. Obedience to God is not an inconvenience, it is our ultimate aspiration; it is not a stumbling block, it is a powerful and profitable building block.

The Healing Power of Forgiveness

Book 4 in The Powerful Christian Series

Repentance and forgiveness are the essence of the gospel of Jesus Christ. It is a principle that offers hope, expectation and encouragement to every believer.

The power of forgiveness brings great joy and peace to us. This infinite miracle is a direct result of the great mediation and atonement of Jesus Christ. This reconciliation, where Jesus through His own choice paid the price of our sins and mistakes, sanctifies and purifies us. It is indeed the greatest miracle of all miracles.

Faith in Jesus Christ teaches us that it is worth everything to continually cleanse and purify our lives through repentance. It is because of our faith in Him that we have the power to receive His forgiveness.

The great blessing and miracle is that you and I have the very same power given to us. It is this inner power of forgiveness that changes lives. We are most like Jesus Christ when we forgive another person.

---

[i] United States Constitution, Amendment 1.

[ii] Millicent J. Taylor, Treasure of Free Men (New York: Harper and Brothers, 1953), p. 71.

[iii] Ibid. p. 72.

[iv] Ernest Christian Helmreich, The German Churches under Hitler (Detroit: Wayne State University Press, 1979), pp. 150, 234, 345, 466.

[v] Carl Carmer, ed., The War against God (New York: Henry Holt and Co., 1943), p. 4.

[vi] Millicent J. Taylor, Treasure of Free Men (New York: Harper and Brothers, 1953), p. 38.

[vii] 6. Eric M. North, ed., The Book of a Thousand Tongues (New York: Harper and Brothers, 1938), p. 13.

www.ingramcontent.com/pod-product-compliance
Lightning Source LLC
Chambersburg PA
CBHW060535030426
42337CB00021B/4278